DREAMING OF A LIFE UNLIVED

Advance Praise For
Dreaming of a Life Unlived

"For too long, the voices of women childless women have been silenced by themselves and by society. Others tend to think that women who don't have children either didn't want them or couldn't have them. The truth is so much more complex and Yvonne's beautiful book is a wonderful introduction to some of those truths. I am immensely proud to be part of it, and to have had the honour of getting to know each of the other women featured."

Jody Day, Founder: Gateway Women

www.gateway-women.com

Dreaming of a life unlived

Intimate stories and portraits of women without children

Yvonne John

Author: Yvonne John
Editor: Margaret Hunter at Daisy Editorial
Cover design: Design for Writers
Cover photo: Shutterstock
Book design: Design for Writers
Images supplied by Yvonne J Photography
Author photograph: SF Digital Studios
Publisher: Yvonne John / www.blurb.co.uk
ISBN 978-1-5262-0121-8

This book includes the author's own account of dealing with child-lessness and grief as well as contributions from other women who she has met. Any personal information in this book has been used with permission. This book is for educational purposes and is not intended to replace medical advice or the services of trained professionals. All the images in this book have been created by the author.

For Selo (Selwyn), Elyse and Annabel

CONTENTS

ACKNOWLEDGEMENTS

To my wonderfully loving husband, David, it has been a hard road and I have been honoured that you chose to stand by my side and hold my hand through it all. Having you here when I felt like I couldn't cry any more helped me to stand one more day. Thank you for choosing me!

To my family and friends (you know who you are), thank you for allowing me to be me.

Thank you to Valerie James for your love, compassion and gentle guidance. You have taught me to stand strong and to sing my song. Without you I would not have realised that I was grieving the loss of my unborn children, and without you I would not have found Gateway Women.

Thank you to Jody Day. If you had not started Gateway Women I would still be lost and would not have found my new family of 'Bees'.

Thank you to Helen Tucker for believing that my story was worth telling.

Thank you to Dee Bailey, who knows how to put a smile on my face. Thanks for all the laughter, love and support.

To my lovely Bees, the Gateway Women community and the beautiful voices in this book (you know who you are), your love and support knows no bounds and this journey would not be the same without you. I hope that this book helps other women find their voices too.

INTRODUCTION

For many women the reality of life without children is one that we never expected to have to face. It wasn't in our life plan and we never imagined that this would happen to us; we never imagined that we wouldn't be mothers. One in five UK women reach their mid-forties without children,[1,] [2] mostly not by choice, and I am one of them. Being on this road is a reality that I have found hard to face. For me it was the start of a painful realisation that I wanted something with my husband that I was never going to have. I wanted to have a family. I thought that I had experienced loss and grief in my life but this was different; it was unexpected, it felt undeserved and yet 'not allowed', because, let's face it, how can you grieve for something that you never had?

So my journey began. A journey of many tears, a journey to understanding, forgiveness and acceptance, a journey of finding my way home. This book is my baby and was conceived among my sister participants on the Gateway Women Plan B mentorship programme. We call ourselves the Gateway Bees and we came together to learn how to grieve and to find ways of being creative in our lives without children. The idea for the book was nurtured and fed with compassion and understanding, and it gave birth to a collection of stories representing women who are standing strong on our journeys towards finding our own Plan B and leading a fulfilling life without children.

I decided that part of my Plan B was to create this book so that those who are not in this place can understand the difficult journey that women who are childless by circumstance are facing. I also wanted to reach out to other women and couples who need that support and hope for their futures. This book is also for their friends and families – who give the essential compassion and support to find a new and satisfying future when life is so muddled and painful.

FINDING MY VOICE

Yvonne John, 45, Married

I remember a time when I felt so low that I couldn't look at my reflection in the mirror. I walked with my head held low, ashamed of who I had become...

Confused and upset, I found myself crying in situations that were previously normal, such as being with my friends and their children, watching young mothers on the train cuddling their babies, listening to women introducing themselves as a mother of three, grandmother of one. I wondered what my children would look like; I secretly wished that I'd have a girl just like me, and wondered if my husband wished for a boy so they could gang up on me. Slowly this became a time of unbearable pain – we never conceived, each month was another terrible disappointment and time was running out for us.

I remember in my early 20s fantasising about being married with four children by the time I was 35, but in the mess of trying to navigate my way through life I somehow lost that dream. As the years went by it became apparent that I wouldn't have four children, and the thought of being this person, a wife and mother, became a scary prospect, so I rejected this dream at almost every opportunity that presented itself.

As I sit here on my birthday, listening to the rain falling outside my window while reflecting on my life, it's hard not to wonder where the last 45 years have gone. I am tempted to start by saying that I was born on a winter's day, I believe that it was snowing, a beautiful baby girl born to two loving parents… but that would be too clichéd. I do have sweet memories of my childhood, which was filled with lots of love and laughter. One of my fondest memories was how secure I felt while sitting on my dad's lap, caressing his beard.

As I headed into my teens I became more aware of the strong messages that my parents wanted to instil in their children. I became conscious of the 'shame' that they believed our potential mistakes could bring on our family. I can't remember if we truly talked as a family. I remember that as children we were told what to do, which I found hard to take, and still do now. During those years I felt like I wasn't seen for who I was – not that I knew who that was – and I didn't have a voice (and I so desperately wanted to be heard, to be seen), which led to arguments and painful encounters with my parents. So I ran off to university in Bristol and spent three years awakening my senses, but mostly throughout my 20s I was trying to find what I had lost , which was that sense of security from my dad that had held me for so many years. Looking back I would have welcomed a script to help me walk through those early years of independence. Something that would have helped me to navigate my way through the confusion of dating, the confusion created by men (of all ages) complementing me on my looks, on my body, telling me what they needed to say to get something from me, something that I wasn't prepared to give away so easily. Throughout my 20s I had some wonderful experiences, but these were few and far between; other experiences often left me feeling disgusted with who I was.

I remember a time when I felt so low that I couldn't look at my reflection in the mirror. I walked with my head held low, ashamed of who I had become, and afraid that if people really knew me they would not like what they saw. I guess this feeling started back in the final year of university. I had recently broken up with my then boyfriend, who I did love and who had loved me back, so I was heartbroken. Being too young to handle these emotions, I ran into the arms of another man with the intention of quickly getting over what I had so recently lost. It was a brief encounter that left me pregnant, with no one to turn to. I felt alone. I was about to take my final exams and should have been excited about my future, but all I could think about was how my life was over. I remember looking at myself in the mirror with contempt, wondering how I was in this mess. All I wanted was for it to end. I felt that I was not brave enough to end my life but didn't know how I was supposed to go on. I didn't believe anyone would feel compassion if I shared my problem, so what was I supposed to do?

I don't know if I would now call it brave or stupid but I decided to terminate the pregnancy; I just wasn't strong enough to be a single mother. I wanted more for me and my child. I wanted the best. I know that I buried my pain and the shame of what I had done in the hope of it all being OK one day, because when that 'one day' came I would be married and have a family, the way it was supposed to be.

During the six years after my first pregnancy I dated many men. I spent those years looking for the love and security I was so desperate to have. I wish I knew who I was back then. If I had known my worth I would have been able to say no without the fear that a man would not like me, or leave when I wanted him to stay. I would have had the strength not to be there in the first place. My confusion continued until I met a man who did bring some hope into my world. We talked, we laughed, and I enjoyed how I felt with him; but he had a girlfriend. We had our night of passion nonetheless (so like a romantic novel), but shortly afterwards he ended what we had because his girlfriend was pregnant. I remember feeling disappointed and abandoned. I remember thinking 'What if I am pregnant too?', but quickly pushed this out of my head. We had used protection, so this could not be true. A week later my worst nightmare became my worst reality. I was again alone, pregnant and scared of the prospect of facing this on my own. My family are very proud so turning to them did not seem like an option for me, as I didn't want to create shame for them. I was so disappointed in myself that I couldn't carry their disappointment too. If only he had chosen me, if only he had said he wanted to have this baby with me... who knows what could have been? After my second termination my life just seemed to spiral out of control. The man told me that he married his girlfriend and I couldn't escape from the thought of how stupid I was to have been in this situation again. Had I not learned from my first mistake? How foolish could I be?

The years that followed seem like a blur. Dating became more difficult as my confusion intensified. I had become lost in what I thought men wanted and was constantly changing myself in the hope that they would stay. I was leapfrogging my way from one relationship to another, becoming more lost with each new experience. Along this road I stumbled into church and spent years hiding from the world with the false promise that my past had been forgiven and was behind me; but I hadn't forgiven myself and I could not forget.

I think I was around 37 years old, two years after leaving the church, when I somehow woke up and really saw who I was. During my time in church I had a place, and to some degree it felt like I had a purpose, until that feeling of security fell apart. I started to notice behaviours that contradicted my values and decided that it was time to leave. When I did I felt lost, depressed and again confused. I felt like I did not know who I was any more. I didn't know my own mind and needed to understand what had led me on this religious path. I started to read books like *Conversations with God*[3] and started questioning what I had previously thought to be true over the past 10 years. Somewhere along this new journey, and for the first time in my life, I was beginning to understand, like and even accept who I was. Somewhere on this journey I decided to stop worrying about what others thought of me and started caring about what I thought of myself instead. I started to like the woman in the mirror as she looked back at me with pride, and the more I liked who I was the more confident I became with the decisions I was making. I had made peace with my past, or so I thought. I just decided that what was done was done and I moved on without questioning my actions. I started to look forward.

I met the man whom I was to marry shortly afterwards. We met at a function where I was hired as a photographer by the organisers. He coolly asked me for my phone number, I responded to his request and we spent the next five months talking, laughing and sharing details of our lives before we even went on our first date. Once we started dating I remember thinking that he really knew me, he showed me a compassion that I had not experienced in a long time, a compassion that melted my heart. We had dated for five wonderful months when he proposed, and it was an easy *yes*. I was amazed at his strength and kindness. He loved me with all my flaws, and he loved me with my past. He made me laugh and in many ways demonstrated qualities that I had only ever seen before in my dad, and I was excited that he was in my life. He wasn't bothered if we had children, and I had already given up on my dream to have them, so we took our vows knowing that our lives would be just the two of us.

"At 40 we started our three year journey of trying to have a baby. I would never have imagined how hard this road would be."

About a year into our marriage we decided to take a leap of faith and see where it would take us. At 40 we started our three-year journey of trying to have a baby. I would never have imagined how hard this road would be, the emotional rollercoaster that took us through calculated liaisons, unspontaneous sex and legs raised in the air for half an hour afterwards, mindlessly flicking through TV channels hoping that this time it had worked, hoping that this time I had conceived. The arguing and months of disappointment are indescribable. I always thought that my husband would welcome the opportunity to have sex whenever it was offered but the forced liaisons left him feeling like a piece of meat. He no longer felt desired or cared for; I just wanted him for his sperm. As he started to lose interest in my advances I became upset that he didn't want to have this baby. Why didn't he want this as much as I did? This part of our journey became very one-sided and I started to resent him for that. I resented him for not wanting our baby as much as I did.

Our lives took another turn when we entered the next phase of our journey, the fertility investigations. I thought that getting pregnant would be easy (it was before), but now it was different: this time I really wanted being pregnant to be my reality. The fertility investigations went on for one year. It was a time of isolation because I didn't tell anyone; it was just me and my husband facing this alone. I couldn't let anyone else know. I just didn't want the pressure of others knowing and asking endless questions about how things were going or if we had any news to tell them. I just didn't feel strong enough to let the world into this very personal part of my life. So with no one to talk to I held on to my husband and took one painful test after another. Each test was followed by months of waiting to see the consultant, and with each consultant's appointment I was left with months of waiting for another test. Where was the urgency, where was the concern that I was 42 and time was not on my side?

I remember sitting in the office of my fertility consultant, after my final fertility test, wondering why he was telling me that he could not find a reason for me not being able to conceive. 'Unexplained infertility,' he said. Hearing it left me feeling so empty and lost. I was confused and just couldn't comprehend him telling me that it might still happen but... 'We can't tell you why it hasn't. It may be your age, as your chances of conception decrease once you hit 40' and 'Why didn't you try sooner?' I so wanted to say 'Why are you asking me these stupid questions?' It felt like he was saying that it would have been better for me to be a single mum rather than wait for my Mr Right. Don't get me wrong, I have nothing against single mums – a part of me so admires their bravery – but bringing up a child while single wasn't for me. Three years and a rather unhelpful consultant later my reality was staring back at me and I had nothing to say. What could I say? I just walked out of his office in a daze, emotionally numb, went home and fell into bed. I was told that I could continue to try naturally or I could consider IVF but as I was 43 I would have to fund this myself. At around £4k - 8k[4] per cycle, with a 4% chance of conceiving, and being in the midst of a very emotional journey, I did not see this as an option for me.

During this time I experienced a range of emotions, from moments of trying to convince myself that 'This will be OK', to moments of crying when seeing my friends and their children, and moments of tears on the train watching young families excited about their day ahead as I realised that I wouldn't get to experience such moments with my own husband or my friends. I experienced moments of anger at hearing how hard it was for friends to conceive a second child after months of trying (because they already had a child!) and after three years all I had was the grief of not being able to conceive. I had moments of shutting my husband out because he couldn't possibly understand how I was feeling. Let's face it, I didn't understand how I was feeling myself, nor why I was crying for no particular reason. I remember sitting with my dad one Sunday afternoon listening to him reminiscing about his grandchildren, and watching the joy on his face reduced me to tears. In that moment I realised that my dad would never have these memories of *my* children, and my children would never have stories of the time they had spent with their granddad. I experienced moments of 'What does this mean for the future of our marriage?' and 'Who will look after us when we get too old to care for ourselves?' I wondered how my husband and I would hold onto our forever after and at the same time I was totally confused about what the hell was happening to me.

Luckily, an older friend, who had been through this too and is also without children, told me I was grieving the loss of my unborn children... WHAT? This made no sense at all. I hadn't lost anything and most importantly I didn't deserve to grieve, not after the way I had lived my life. Not after the choices that I had made. I wasn't even sure if I truly wanted children. But I came to realise that I *was* grieving. I was grieving the loss of what had passed and the loss of the children that would never be.

It has been tough trying to comprehend this grief. At first it seemed unreal – how could this be grief? But my friend told me about the organisation called Gateway Women and I attended a living without children workshop. Slowly I began to comprehend and started the Gateway Women Plan B programme on 8th March 2015.

So somehow I have arrived here, grieving this loss, and have found Jody Day and Gateway Women. They have pretty much saved my sanity. It has been difficult to fully grieve, especially as my husband hasn't shown any signs of this loss too. In some ways I felt that I was being unfair to our relationship because part of me was grieving for the loss of the pregnancy I terminated nearly 10 years ago. This wasn't my husband's past, so how could he be a part of this grief? On the other hand I resented him for not feeling the loss of the child we had tried to conceive for three years. It felt like this didn't matter to him and at times I realised that he didn't understand why I was so upset. What was also unhelpful were the endless questions from people such as 'Have you considered adoption?' and 'What about IVF?' Dealing with these questions was difficult, especially when presented from unfamiliar faces. No one asked how I was feeling or acknowledged how hard this must be for me. The truth is, when I was younger I thought that if the time came and adoption or IVF were my only options to have a child then I would jump at the chance, but now that I am here, facing this with my husband, I know that this wouldn't be the right choice for us. As a result of such questions I found myself doubting if I did want a child, because if I did I should have tried everything in my power to make this happen. But I realised that I needed to, wanted to, deal with my grief. For me, adopting a child would have just covered the sadness, and going through IVF would not only have put a financial burden on our relationship but would have delayed the grief that I was so desperate to understand. So I chose to stay and face what was in my heart.

One of the first steps I took on this journey of healing was to learn to finally forgive myself for my past. Through Gateway Women I realised that I was no longer alone and was able to work towards understanding the decisions behind terminating my pregnancies. I wanted the best for my children and couldn't bring them into my chaotic world. I spoke to myself as if I was speaking to a friend who was going through the situation (instead of me), and I spoke to myself with a compassion and a gentleness that I had not used before, which was so comforting that it helped me to heal this part of my hurt.

I realise that my grief will always remain with me, but with each day it is becoming easier to deal with as the scars of my past begin to heal. For the most part I am now OK, but there are moments that pick at my scar, moments that will still bring tears to my eyes. I used to tell myself that I had made mistakes, but now I see that I simply made choices – choices that others will judge me for, but no more than I have judged myself.

My darling Regina
Please know that you were loved and
desired and will always have a special
place in my heart. You were named
after your granddad Reginald, who
would have been so proud of you,
just as we, your parents, would have
been.
I dreamed of you so many times,
crawling onto your dad's lap while he
was studying and lying on his chest as you
both slept on a hot summer's day.
You were a part of my thoughts
for so long that it broke my heart
to know that you would never be, that
I'd never get to know you or see who
you would become.
I wish I could have known you with your dad and seen you
share your granddad's memories. I wish I could have seen your smile
and heard you laugh. I wish I could have held you in my arms when you
cried. I wished so much for you. You will always be in my thoughts.
Your Loving Mum xxx

*A letter to my unborn child as part of my grief work on Jody Days' Plan B
Mentorship Programme*

Working towards and through acceptance

has led me to another type of **hope**.

A hope that will see me finding my

'purpose' and a sense of **fulfillment.**

Not in the way I had always thought I

would.

But knowing that there is something out

there for me,

another path that I can pursue and another

way to feel **happy**,

gives me a small sense of **excitement**.

And for me, this feeling of excitement is

getting **stronger** each day[5]

BLACK DOG CLUB

Heather Boyd-Savidge, 39, Married

"My dogs are my lifeline, my consistent companions, always beside me, helping me to love life again."

W e have all seen guide dogs, hearing dogs and dogs for the disabled, but what about dogs for the broken-hearted?

I hadn't realised until recently that my first love was my dog. We called her Bouncer and she became my best friend. She provided me with lots of fun and adventure as a young teenager. I was 12 years old turning 13 and feeling vulnerable, scared, unsure and worried about being accepted at a new school, along with the pressures of changing from a girl to a woman. Bouncer accepted me wholeheartedly, regardless of my mood, appearance or what I was wearing. I didn't need to worry about fitting in with her around.

I met my amazing husband at 22. We met at work, where I was the new receptionist and he was the new CAD technician. He had an abundance of energy, fun, love and understanding. I knew straight away he was the man for me. The first present I ever bought him was a pair of wellies so he could join me and Bouncer on muddy walks through the countryside. We fell in love across fields, woods and walks with the dog.

We bought our first house in 2006 when I was 30 years old. As soon as we moved in we started planning for a family of our own. Patiently waiting for something to happen, my periods were like clockwork. I looked after my body, I was young, fit, healthy and happy. Then very suddenly late in 2009 everything changed. I had six weeks of hot flushes. I just thought it was a phase. Then my periods would come every three months. Every time I missed a period I thought I was pregnant. But I wasn't; the tests came back negative. I was diagnosed with early menopause at the start of 2011. I felt completely heartbroken, shocked and in absolute disbelief that having my own children with my husband was not a possibility.

Very soon after my diagnosis my sister offered to be an egg donor. She was fit, healthy and already had two of her own children, and the clinic said she sounded ideal. Hope was not lost, and my husband and I agreed that this would be an alternative solution. We quickly got appointments and tests organised for my sister. The clinic identified that her egg quality was not good enough and the chance of egg donation being successful was very slim. I couldn't believe it – another massive blow in the space of a month. My sister was devastated.

Offers from other egg donors came later, but by this point we couldn't cope with any more false hope. We decided to take a break and remind ourselves of who we were.

This was closely followed by the loss of my Dad in 2011, which left me at breaking point. Trapped in a lonely and isolating place, broken by pain and despair, I couldn't carry on any more. I wanted to give up on life. Feeling broken-hearted and written off, I had lost myself in grief, guilt and sadness.

By this point in my life I had three dogs, all black, Bob, Diesel and Cookie. I called them the Black Dog Club. The expressive ears, wagging tails, eyes full of love and endless amounts of cuddles kept me company. Knowing I had to nurture and care for them gave me a sense of purpose. I was never on my own, I had to get up, I had to put one step in front of the other, I had to embrace nature, wind, sun and rain and the routine of the changing seasons. They gave me a purpose and provided an abundance of unconditional love in an absolutely devastating chapter of my life.

The road to recovery has been tough. I have worked through my pain, by a combination of counselling and finding the tribe of Gateway Women. But my dogs have been there for me time and again, and have saved me by acceptance, love, energy and humour. They are my lifeline, my consistent companions, always beside me, helping me to love life again.

How do you explain **a loss you never had**?

Yvonne

BREAKING THE SILENCE

Lucia E Melillo, 45, Living with partner

"I was so lonely and felt like no-one understood how I was feeling."

'W'hy are you not married? I cannot believe it.'

'You have no children, how come? You're Italian. You Italians are all good at eating and shagging and having loads of children!'

'Do you want children?'

'Must be something wrong there – she is on her own all this time.'

'Well, she is married to her business. She wouldn't have time for a family.'

For as long as I can remember I have been asked questions about why I do not have children, which has left me feeling isolated and inadequate. There was one memorable Christmas get-together filled with friends, their partners and, of course, their children. The conversations centred around catching up on their lives and talking about how wonderful their families are. I got the impression that they were competing with each other about how successful they had become with their perceived perfect families. It was becoming unbearable. I noticed someone's children being loud and refusing to sit at the table when dinner was served. 'I wouldn't let my boys do that,' said one over-opinionated friend. She always seems to have a lot to say about her own skills as a mother.

Being there at that time listening to those comments was hard as I was beginning to feel like a right failure for not being like them, for not having a child of my own. The conversation seemed to quickly turn to me as I was asked, 'So Lucia, when are you going to meet someone? You know you should if you want children' and 'How old are you now?' All these personal questions about my life – who do they think they are? I felt hurt and angry. Why did they think that they had the right to be this nosey? I felt like they were judging me, and at the same time I felt like I was judging myself. I started to question if I had failed in my life because of not having children, and I couldn't even tell them how it felt. When it became too much I made my excuses and retreated back to the safety of my home, alone with my thoughts.

Coming from a typical Italian family, where my mother was one of 10 and my dad was one of who knows how many, it was expected that I would in turn have lots of children of my own. My parents left Italy in search of a new life as the economy declined after the Second World War. They wanted to leave it all behind, including their families and the traditions that came with it. When I started school I began to adopt English culture. I did not like the restrictions of an Italian upbringing and wanted to be free like some of my peers; but this left me feeling lost and unsure about which culture I truly belonged to. I felt like I had lost out on a family in England and a family of my own. It was a confusing time as part of me wanted a life filled with excitement, travel and fun and part of me felt that I should marry and settle down.

I can remember when I found out I was pregnant (October 2003). I had been so busy with my fundraising activities, which took me around the world exploring exciting places. It was hard but I was breaking the mould of my Italian culture. Returning from one of my treks, I remember realising that I had not had a period for a couple of months so I took a home pregnancy test. I was apprehensive about the result and at the same time didn't think that I could possibly be pregnant but thought I would rule it out anyway. When I saw that positive line on the test I was instantly happy, which lasted for all of five minutes when I was hit with the reality that the father was not with me. We had broken up around two to three weeks before after the realisation that he did not care about starting a family with me as he already had a daughter. I felt lost as I sat alone wondering what I was going to do. I started to query if I could be a single mother and how I would cope. After a couple of days I plucked up the courage to call him with my news. This was difficult as he initially didn't believe me and insisted on seeing the test. It took a while to convince him of the reality of this, at which point we started to discuss the situation. It soon became clear that he couldn't cope and I started to see that he was a child himself. I wanted to give up work but he was angry at this suggestion because I earned more than him, which led to row after row. What should have been a happy event started to quickly turn into a nightmare. I felt alone and torn between wanting to be with him and wondering how I would manage on my own.

With my uncertainties in tow I went for my first scan. I was around 18 to 20 weeks and feeling apprehensive as they put the cold gel on my belly, turned on the monitor and rubbed the ultrasound transducer across my stomach to get a picture of what was growing inside of me. As the image appeared and I became curious the nurse quickly turned the monitor away without any explanation. What was happening? I became frightened as a doctor appeared. He poked and prodded around then told me that my baby hadn't formed properly. I was so traumatised that this started to become a blur. I couldn't comprehend what was happening as the doctor continued to speak. This felt unreal as I tried to grasp onto reality. I can't remember what happened next or how I even got home, but I do remember around three days later standing in my bath-room and feeling drained. I felt an intense pain in my stomach, which took me back to the hospital. Once again I was in a blur and in what felt like minutes my baby was gone. I can't say how I felt, who was there or how I got home, but I do remember sitting in my front room with my relatives staring back at me, no one saying a word. I think the worst part of this was being with the people who were supposed to care about me but who didn't know what to say. There were no words of comfort, no one said 'I'm sorry' or asked 'How are you feeling?' Once again I felt alone.

It took at least a year to get over this experience. I no longer had a partner and had lost my baby. I was so lonely and felt like no one understood how I was feeling. 'It was not meant to be', 'You'll meet someone else', 'Go to a sperm bank and have one on your own', 'Well at least it happened now and not later on' was the only consolation I received from people, with smiles on their faces, laughing and joking at my expense. I looked at them and felt like this was another thing that I had to deal with, as if the loss of my baby wasn't enough. It was like a silent sadness that cannot be spoken about and that others cannot bear to hear or feel. All my plans and hopes gone, a sad secret that I carried around with me for about a year.

One of the things that helped me to recover from my loss was resuming my plans to take a counselling course. I felt reborn as I studied and underwent personal therapy. I began to feel listened to and for the first time felt like someone understood how I was feeling inside. I did not have to shy away from what was painful and unfair. I finally felt supported. I began learning a new language, one that was more thoughtful, kind and non-judgemental, which was liberating.

Eight years on and at 42 I met Paul through an introduction agency. I felt ready to date but wanted to meet a special someone. Paul was kind, gentle and thoughtful and so different from what I had known before. We dated for four months and it was clear to me that he was reliable; I felt safe. At 41 Paul, like me, didn't have children. It did feel sad that we hadn't met 10 years sooner and explored the possibility of having children together, but we reflected positively on our situation. We dated for three years before Paul moved in. I felt complete, I felt like I belonged. I enjoyed planning a future with Paul.

I still feel sad when I reflect on my past, but I do feel that my life is full without children. I no longer judge myself and am a lot kinder to myself. I now choose not to listen to women going on and on about their parental skills as I have learned that there are many roads. They all give different experiences and mine are certainly not less because I am childless. I believe that it takes a brave person to be different.

This is the **first** new year that I've entered

with **hopes** of having my own family put

firmly behind me,

and I am learning to **accept**

(and perhaps even enjoy)

where I am right now[5]

HIDING AWAY

Tracey, 40, Single

'That strange, awkward lady who never opens up about herself.' If I could read other people's minds, I'm sure that's what I would hear if they were to describe me. Quiet, evasive and reserved – that's how it feels like they see me.

I don't blame them, because that's probably how I come across.

But I'd love for someone to stop and ask themselves why. Has anyone ever tried to see beyond their initial assumptions of me? Have they stopped and thought about whether it is their own preconceived ideas of what a 40-year-old woman should be like that has encouraged someone like me to stay quiet and hide away?

If those people did take a moment to look beyond this exterior, what would they see? They'd see a woman whose heart has broken because the lifelong dream she held for years never became a reality. They'd see a woman who struggles to navigate everyday life because of the constant reminders around her of what didn't happen. The dream of someday becoming a mother.

Over the years the words 'When I have kids' gradually changed to 'If I have kids', to what is now a silence where words were once spoken. To me this silence is piercing. It follows me everywhere. It's there when I'm at work, it's there when I'm at home, it's there when I'm socialising. It's there wherever I go. There is no escaping it. I am a childless woman living in a world where most of my peers are married and most have kids. I'm the odd one out. I'm the one who finds it difficult to join in conversations about those everyday matters that everyone else seems to be talking about – kids, partners, in-laws.

And that was never my plan. It wasn't meant to turn out like this. It never crossed my mind that I wouldn't meet a suitable partner to settle down and have a family with. No way, not me! According to friends and family – those who know me well – I have loads going for me. And that's what I believed. It would happen, when it happened. Except it never did. The day I realised that was the day a part of me broke inside. And because part of me broke, I began to hurt. And because it hurts, I want to look after it. Protect it. That's what makes me hide such a big part of me away.

But that same realisation also forced me to seek out help and support. Over the past year I have begun to work on this with a wonderful group of women I met through Gateway Women, who have all faced similar experiences to myself. I have found this enormously helpful, so much so that the silence I described as piercing is now gradually becoming duller and I'm beginning to find my place in the world again. I'm not there yet, but the journey has definitely begun.

I am

learning to accept that life didn't turn out as

I'd hoped.

I am

learning to accept that my future won't look

the same as I had imagined when I was

younger.

I am

learning to accept that my life has taken a very

different path to most of my friends and family.

But most of all

I am

learning to accept

myself[5]

20TH AUGUST 2013, 11:55PM ROME

Sam Bragg, 42, Married

"Initially our sex life was exciting but it slowly started to diminish... I tried sexy undies, silky underwear... with no result"

The end of a fantastic day. My husband and I had just been to *La Traviata*, an amazing opera. It was a warm evening and we stopped for a glass of champagne in a pavement restaurant, watching the world go by. So romantic and everything I could have wished for. Five minutes to go and it was the start of a 'special' birthday – my 40th. The minutes slowly ticked away, midnight arrived, we clinked glasses and... the floodgates opened. My husband didn't understand what was happening. This was supposed to be a happy moment, not a blot on our memories forever.

Looking back, I know that by staying up late that evening I was trying to extend being 39 for as long as possible. Realistically, I know that age is only a number, but 40 was my brick wall. Suffering from chronic fatigue and pain symptoms, I had no energy left in me to climb the wall, let alone knock it over. My 12-year longing for a child had come to an end as hope was killing me.

My dreams since teenage years had always included having the perfect family. One husband and one child (I wasn't going to be greedy). Living in a country cottage and nurturing my baby boy named Archie (taking my grandfather's name into a future generation). Our life a cross between the couples in *The Good Life* sitcom. My father taught me to grow vegetables, and I too was going to nourish my family, producing home-grown goodies like Tom and Barbara, but with the social life and elegance of Margo and Jerry.

I met my husband through work and although 15 years my senior he was young at heart. I just knew he was my Mr Perfect. We holidayed, partied and enjoyed life. Following marriage I didn't want children immediately. I wanted to revel in being Mr and Mrs for a while and had age 28 in mind to add the 'plus one' to our unit. I am not a spontaneous person and wanted security before jumping into family life. Initially our sex life was exciting, but it slowly started to diminish and impotency issues ensued. I tried sexy undies, silky under-wear… with no result. As an anxious perfectionist with low self-esteem, I took his lack of desire as being my fault. I felt that I was fat, unattractive, unsexy, unfeminine, and always assumed that maybe someone else was providing his pleasure. I checked my fertility cycle, and if the luxury of intimacy happened I was always hopeful, but 'mother nature' stabbed me in the back at every opportunity.

Years passed and the subject of SEX became the elephant in the room between us and physical contact was distant. We had more of a sibling relationship than marital. I didn't want to constantly nag so withheld inner thoughts and feelings rather than communicate. Everyone around me seemed to be dropping children like rabbits, so obviously their partners were content with them. I was ashamed and afraid to talk to friends about the subject as I felt that I had to appear 'strong', 'normal' and 'happy'. I compared myself to everyone's positive aspects and felt weak, inadequate and incredibly resentful for their success and 'perfect lives'. Putting on a false facade to go out became the norm, and making excuses for not attending social events was a safe thing to do. It helped me avoid the inevitable questions: 'Do you have children?', 'Why not?', 'Why don't you try IVF or adopt?' Blah blah blah.

Following my 40th, and the imminent birth of my first niece/nephew, I withdrew both physically and emotionally from as much of life as possible, including family. I did what I had to do to survive and hid away behind closed doors. Until, that is, October 2014, a date that strongly resonates with me. A close friend had rather upset me with an insensitive comment. I typed 'HELP I'm childless' into a search engine and up popped Gateway Women. The tears of relief flowed, knowing I was not alone with these thoughts and feelings. There are times when I don't feel I would be here today had I not found this website or met some fantastic childless women, with incredible heart-wrenching stories, who are making me feel worthwhile and part of society again.

With the realisation my husband is fast approaching 58, and with health and medical issues for us both, including problem sperm, I realise that I no longer have the strength to manage the responsibilities that a young child brings. Yes, I know Rod Stewart and Michael Douglas have done it – I've been told so many times – but let's be reasonable here: they do get a lot of help! My bubble of 'hope' has now popped! After nearly 15 years of mentally attacking myself, these feelings of inadequacy and the constant self-berating *have* to stop. I don't have it in me to bonk the recommended twice a day kindly suggested by the doctor just in case one of the 'problem tadpoles' can get through, nor the strength to go through an adoption process. Having removed myself from being close to children over the course of the past 10 years, I am not sure I would be able to bond with another person's child. IVF is a route I have never felt comfortable with, perhaps because of what it puts your body through or the artificial nature of it. It doesn't mean I disagree with either of these options. They work for some but are just not part of who I am. I am no longer going to feel guilty for these thoughts.

So it's time to move on and find a different direction to the one I had originally planned. My husband has now admitted that children were not necessarily part of his own goals but he would have welcomed change had we been lucky. Having undertaken both personal and couples psychosexual counselling for the last two+ years, this is the start of my Plan B. We were not naturally able to conceive so are now working to build a new life together without the children I had so strongly desired. Focus for me has to be towards building a stronger bond between us and experiencing a feeling of contentment and inclusion.

As my love for my husband grew,

my desire to add to

our family grew[6]

THE ASIAN BLACK SHEEP

Vivian, 44, married

"We put all our hopes into the final attempt with our frozen embryos... Somehow this was going to be the one."

So, auntie and uncle have spoken to a specialist doctor and decided that because of your long-term medical conditions you shouldn't have children.'

It brought a tear to my eye, a lump to my throat. I wanted to scream. I just made it out of the room before the floodgates opened, and all I could do was sit in the bathroom and sob. Who were they to decide my future and my life?

Ask me how I am, if I'm OK, if I'm well. Ask me if we are having problems conceiving. Ask me how the IVF is going. Tell me you're sorry about the miscarriage I have had. But don't say nothing. Don't gossip, don't make up your own version of events. Ask me – I'm human.

It's a common assumption that as soon as you're married, the next step is automatically having babies. If it hasn't happened within two years, the rumour mill begins. For me, the phone calls began... 'Any good news?' 'So, anyone got any good news going on, anything to tell us?' By 'any good news' it was quite obvious that it was the words 'We are pregnant' that people were after.

Our journey of wanting a child, like most couples, began a couple of years after we got married. We were trying for a baby, and in fact trying everything that is supposed to help: putting your legs up in the air after sex, putting a pillow under your bum after sex... We went on holiday, hoping that chilling out lying on a beach and being relaxed would help somehow. Every month there was hope that this time it would work, yet every month there was heartache. And so, month after month, the wanting grew more and more.

After a year of trying, we went to the GP and asked for help. And so began our journey of trying to find out why we hadn't yet been able to conceive. After being poked and prodded and having bloods done for every test under the sun, I was given the 'unexplained fertility' tag. The word 'unexplained' is the most annoying word in the world! *Why* could they not explain? What we weren't expecting was to be told that my hubby had a low sperm count and low motility, meaning that the only realistic way we could conceive would be through IVF. It's a bit of a shock to a man being told this news; not quite what he or I were expecting. Secretly I was thinking that at least it wasn't all my fault! It's human nature to assume it must be the woman's fault.

Our first venture into IVF filled us with hope for our big chance. Through every blood test, every time I spread my legs for another test or another doctor to examine me, which was all very humiliating, all we could think of was this could result in our baby. The initial treatment began with painful injections. Stabbing yourself every day with the drugs is no fun, leaving you sore and in so much pain. After a few weeks of injections, and having regular scans too, we were then told that I was a 'non-responder'. My body wasn't reacting to the drugs the way it should do. We sat in the clinic and were told 'You'll never have kids'. Most of the rest of that day is a blur. I remember calling work and saying I wouldn't be in. I recall going home on the train and doing my best not to cry, holding back till the minute I got through the door of my flat. Then the tears just didn't stop.

I felt alone, facing the reality of childlessness.

Somehow my hubby and I got through this pain. I think you end up blocking out everything that you have been through. We were told to try another clinic and another consultant. The new consultant was a bit more promising. Though I was a non-responder or slow responder to treatment, I was told that there was still hope. They'd try different medication and they would alter the dose too. And so began another journey into IVF.

I spent two weeks travelling to central London prior to work at ungodly hours for scans and blood tests. Sitting waiting, watching other couples going through the same thing as me. Just that ache of wanting a hand to hold, a hug, a loving smile. But no, I was on my own. My hubby had said he'd come to the important appointments but this was another lonely day at the hospital. Another day at work with not a single person knowing my traumatic experiences before I even got to work. I felt so lonely. I wanted to go to work and say 'Look, this is what I'm dealing with', but there were so many women at work either pregnant or with young babies, which made it too difficult. All conversations seemed to be about babies and pregnancies, and it just didn't feel right to tell my story. I guess I didn't want the sympathetic sighs or hugs or to make it uncomfortable for people to talk about their kids or pregnancy without feeling sorry for me.

The first wait for the call to say yes it's positive or sorry it's negative is the worst, the longest and the loneliest wait in the world. 'It's weakly positive,' she said. Was I hearing correctly? She said it's positive! It was almost disbelief. Our first attempt, and it worked! My hubby and I were elated, but he was more cynical, and wasn't getting too excited just yet. I guess he was waiting for the first scan, which would make it a bit more real. But your mind still goes into overdrive, and you start planning baby names and the future for you and your child. There were calls of congratulations from the few friends who knew – welcome to sleepless nights and nappy days. Was it real? I even bought my hubby a birthday card from baby and me.

But 10 more days and then 'I'm sorry, there's no heartbeat' during the scan. Disbelief. I went home and pretended that nothing had happened. I went to work, carried on with normal family and home life, pretended that my heart was not broken, just tried to get through the day without crying. Sitting with work colleagues for lunch, where the only topic of conversation was pregnancy, babies, pictures, just got too much, and yet I felt I would be rude if I got up and left the table. I was suffering the heartache along with the immense pain of a miscarriage.

Three more attempts followed, but none with a positive result. We put all our hopes into the final attempt with our frozen embryos. I had reflexology, was chilled and relaxed, with a positive mental attitude. Somehow this was going to be the one. I was quite positive about this attempt, so much so that my hubby went on a lad's holiday. The call came: 'Sorry, it's negative.' I had to call my hubby abroad, but couldn't get through to him, I so clearly remember the message I left with my brother-in-law, the message was that the 'house sale' did not go through! Taking that final fateful call at home alone, that was the end. My body had had enough, my heart couldn't be broken any more, I was alone and the reality of childlessness hit home.

We were an Asian childless couple – what a taboo.

We've had all the stock responses. We were told to adopt a child because we are the last generation and would have no one to carry on the family name. We've been offered all kinds of plants to grow, drugs to try, tablets to take, statues to worship. Someone also felt bad that we didn't have kids and so we were suddenly godparents to three children half way through our marriage. We love them to bits, don't get me wrong, but if we had kids of our own I'm sure that wouldn't have happened. They are my 'sympathetic children'.

However, at no point did anyone ever say, 'Are you both OK?' 'Are you struggling with conception?' 'Is there anything we can do to help?' 'Do you need help with anything?' That's what I'd have liked to have been asked, as opposed to people saying nothing and talking behind our backs... and I know for a fact that was happening.

Life for me now means feeling the odd one out anywhere I go.

At girly dinners not being able to talk about what uni my kids are going to, what they are up to.

Not being invited to mums' nights out from school just makes me feel so alienated.

The heartache of not seeing my own mum being a grand-mummy.

The wanting of a hug from a child saying 'I love you, mummy'.

I just feel so lost and lonely. I don't fit in with the mummy crowd; I'm too old to hang out with the younger generation. I feel like I still to this day don't fit in anywhere.

I hate being the social outcast. People think if you don't have kids, what will we talk about? I find women the worst. No child seems to equal no life in some people's eyes!

I do have a life and a loving husband, and I still have a few great friends who understand my pain. I still have a crazy social life. Life still goes on even without children.

It's amazing that I had forgotten how much I had gone through until I started writing this piece. It still hurts, almost 10 years after my final treatment. The want of and longing for a child will never end, and the reality is that I will always be the 'Asian black sheep'.

I said **goodbye** to the dream of having my

own family.

The words

'my time will come'

became gradually **quieter**

in my head.

The sentence,

'When I have children…',

that once used to slip out

so easily in conversation with others,

disappeared[5]

COMING HOME

Genevieve Smyth, 44, Living with partner

"Here is Melody, sweet as a song, and Ed, sharp as a needle, and my tiny Rose, who wants to be a bear when she grows up."

try to breathe calmly in the bare, grey room. Anxious
sweat on my upper lip, dreading the question from this
new doctor.

'Pregnancies?' I let the air flow gently into my body.

'Three', I reply 'and three miscarriages.' I exhale. I watch
her, waiting for the response.

'Sorry,' she mumbles as she taps on her computer. No eye
contact. I feel my children between us brushing my skin
with their quiet feathers.

So, doctor, will you acknowledge my children, my family?
Here is Melody, sweet as a song, and Ed, sharp as a needle, and
my tiny Rose, who wants to be a bear when she grows up. Can
you measure their height and weight in my heart?

Can you record in my notes that I'm an expert in miscarriage?
Earned through blood like a fierce tide, soaking my clothing,
drowning my dreams, pouring like a tragic storm. I am immersed
in the plasma of my children. They swim towards me with salty
kisses.

Can you recognise in your notes that my grief is an absolute
fire that extends before me and closes after me? I watch with
despair as the flames are fed by assumption and exclusion. I am
learning to fire walk, my children like hot salamanders hissing
in the sky.

Can you test and diagnose how far I have burrowed into the soil to survive? Planting my children in the mulch that is ploughed, refined and mixed. It is so precious a warm, dark place. I rock myself as if comforting a grizzly baby, a dejected child.

Can you advise of any treatment to heal my soul? For the next woman who sits in this tired room with an invisible family? For your friend or your sister who did not have those much-longed-for children?

We sit in brief silence. You offer me nothing at all: a depressingly familiar pattern I am learning to challenge. So instead of emptiness, can I offer you this gift instead? Prepare your prescription pad for our medicine, our remedy for the alleviation of a much-ignored and misunderstood condition.

First is to prescribe breathing again. Women can hold their breath for many years, freezing the body to lock out the pain. Mindful breathing, relaxed breathing, calming, grounding breathing. Air is a healer. So simple and profound, our lungs are gateways to clarity and peace.

Second is to prescribe feeling again. To open to pain. Sense the fear, loss, guilt, shame. Meet it with gentleness and compassion. Discern the shape and size of a weary spirit. To be a kind friend to feelings. To be a good support to the soul. Our hearts beating strong, keeping us alive.

Third is to prescribe dreaming again. To reignite fire and passion. To find faith where it is lost. To peek at the world from under the burden of sadness and take small, shy steps to inspiration. Our feet carrying us to new desires.

And last you need to prescribe the earth and humankind again. To find others who sing the same song, beat the same drum. We are living in your street, in your town, in your country all over the world RIGHT NOW. To share our stories. To realise it's not our fault. To learn to come home to ourselves.

I'm a long way from my where

I want to be,

but

I am happy that **I am taking**

these small steps in the

right direction[5]

IT

Natasha Ascott, 43, Married on the 25th June 2016

I didn't recognise 'IT'. Why would I? Being childless is OK, isn't it? I can have lots of holidays, a fantastic career and lots of free time. That's what everyone would answer if I was brave enough to tell them. But it's not OK.

It took me a long time to find the man that I finally wanted to have a family with. Things didn't happen naturally and we ended up having three unsuccessful cycles of IVF. We even had viable embryos for freezing and transferring at a later stage. Sadly, we were unsuccessful and after eight years of being on an emotional rollercoaster we decided to try no more. Initially I was relieved and life carried on. I threw myself back into work, bought lots of new things to make me feel better and booked an amazing holiday. You see, being a health care professional, I was used to protecting myself from emotional trauma and had built up quite a barrier. It took me at least six months to recognise that I'd lost my smile and that my life continued to go along with me looking in from the outside, to recognise why facing another day without a purpose was eating away at me. I was pretty horrid to people, especially those I loved and cared about, but even more I was very harsh on myself.

It was only during a holiday in Argentina, while walking on the glaciers, that I recognised 'IT'. The sticking plasters would work no more and there, faced with one of the most beautiful sites in the world, my own world fell apart. Ironic really. As the shafts of ice broke away and fell into the sea, a phenomenon known as calving, so did my barriers dissolve to reveal my shattered heart. I had finally recognised that 'IT' was grief. Grief for the loss of something invisible to others, grief for never becoming a mother and grief for never having a family with the man I love. Most of all grief for not knowing what to do with all the love that I had saved for my longed-for son or daughter.

The past year has been tough, with a spectrum of different emotions, and I realise I still have a way to go. Finding Gateway Women made me realise that I'm not on my own, and for that I will always be grateful. It's no longer all negative; in fact, that deep dark grey cloud of grief is now a lighter shade of silver, and its even been known to glimmer with kind words and compassion.

So now that I have trusted you with my story, don't feel

awkward, and please don't try to fix it. Just acknowledge how hard it has been. I don't expect you to recognise 'IT' either. How could you, when I didn't?

Despite your best efforts

life doesn't turn out as you hoped, know that

there is **something**

else out there waiting for you,

something just as **big** and just as

exciting.

And part of the **adventure** is

finding what that is[5]

AT LEAST KNOW MY NAME BEFORE YOU TALK TO MY VAGINA

April Clifford, 45

"I'd forgotten about the toy house that I had put away in my loft. Taking it out again brought back some painful memories"

I have lived my life, as a general rule of thumb, getting to know someone prior to showing them my vagina. The grand unveiling usually follows a few drinks, a few jokes, some more drinks, gambling on the choice of sex music, and a bloody good snog. However, going through fertility treatment forced me to adopt a much more slutty approach to life with my vagina. More of a laissez-faire 'My name's April and this is my vagina' approach in fact. No small talk about my day so far, just 'Take your knickers off and lie down behind that curtain please'.

In all fairness, perhaps I'm being rather harsh to those professionals. Vaginal familiarisation over facial recognition must be an occupational hazard in this particular line of work. The job necessitates a choice – face or fanny – and in this scenario the entrance to my vagina took centre stage. I considered buying ping-pong balls to bring an air of cabaret to the proceedings, but I didn't think the effort would get the credit it deserved. I mean, what other approach could the medical staff realistically take? If they had offered me a glass of Pinot Grigio and a 'knock knock' joke at the start of the appointment I think it would have crossed a line none of us would have been comfortable with.

Three rounds of IVF made the task of keeping an air of mystery and intrigue about my vagina impossible. It involved more tests than I care to remember, and each of those tests required at least one person peering into my vagina. I lost track of who had and hadn't seen it; not a predicament I had previously found myself in. The thing that was possibly most alarming was that, while only a few of them could have picked my face out in a police line-up, I'm sure they could all have identified my fanny from fifteen feet!

In their position I doubt I'd have time to get to know both me and my vagina either. After all, during each round of IVF I was one of many women going through it. A never-ending procession of vaginas working hard to fulfil their potential, while attempting to retain their integrity under the harsh spotlight of the internal investigation. It's enough to test the bond between any woman and her vagina.

So what's our relationship like now? I'm still really rather fond of my vagina. We've been through a lot together: good times (that would be telling), bad times (I could give cystitis a miss) and WTF times (that first and every subsequent period). IVF is a fucking bitch, but my vagina and I have stayed friends long after the medical professionals couldn't remember my name.

"99.9% of me knows' that I will not be a

mother

but

0.1% is still hopeful.

That 0.1% is **so hard to let go**

of but

maybe that's because I am **too**

scared to let go."

April

REFLECTION
DECEMBER 2015

Ellen, 47, Single

"My life felt so desperately sad and empty. Alone, single, miles from home and never to have a family of my own."

Another year nearly reaches its conclusion. As I look back it has had its moments, asking or rather demanding me to find my status in the world.

A single woman, 47, in pretty damned good shape, good job, confident, capable, independent, courageous and lovable, despite some grumpy tendencies. And yet at times I feel so lost. As I try to carve my purpose in life, sometimes I feel so very single and so very alone. I have everything in life I could want, I'm by no means wealthy but financially free of burden, and yet I am missing the two things most people take for granted: romantic love and a family of my own.

Why? The question is heavy and troublesome to me. So many reasons, and a result of various twists and turns – choosing to take one path when two are presented and ending up on the one that has finally led me to this place.

It had never been top of mind for me, having a family. Emigrating to New Zealand at the age of 15 gave me a single focus and the drive and determination to return to England to live the life I felt I had been deprived of by my moving 12,000 miles across the earth. Eight years later, and a double degree in my pocket, I was ready to go and live the life I felt I had left behind.

Boyfriends weren't top of mind either. I was a somewhat shy teenager, and still am shy with men, though most would laugh if I told them that. I felt inhibited by my more confident, older sister, who had a natural rapport with the opposite sex. I always felt I operated in the shadows, that I was a bit of an ugly duckling, and so developed an outer protective shell that would give the impression of confidence, disinterest and nonchalance towards men. It led to a series of odd boyfriend choices, all of whom, in hindsight, were totally not right for me.

It wasn't until I was in my second year of university that I finally embarked on my first real relationship. I then spent most of my 20s doing everything I could to avoid pregnancy. It wasn't in my life plan. Yet.

In my late 20s I met a man I thought I would love forever. Quiet, mysterious and slightly moody, he was in many ways opposite to me. I recall his mother saying to me I had helped make him into a human being again. He had always told me of his strong aversion to marriage and that he didn't want kids. At 28 nor did I, and marriage really wasn't something I aspired to. As I reached my mid-30s, however, I thought about family life more and more. I wanted to give a child the love and joy I had experienced myself. I thought our children would be beautiful, well rounded and good people, and here I was with the man I loved, 10 years into my career and our own home.

I remember sitting in a bar near Baker Street after work one day and raising the possibility of a family with him. His reaction hurt me deeply: 'Next you'll be wanting to get married.' I think I replied 'And why not?', to which he rolled his eyes and the subject was closed. Tony was not a talkative man. At several points over the next four years I would raise the subject again, though rarely did the conversation last. Then at 38 I had had enough. In December 2006 I gave him an ultimatum. He needed to decide what he wanted by the New Year, otherwise I would be gone. New Year came and went, but this time I had my exit strategy in place and a cold and hardened resolve. On the 16th of January I sat him down and told him I was leaving. It was too late and I was moving out. I told him if I reached the age of 45 having been denied the right to have a family by him I would hate him. I left a week later. He didn't put up a fight and he didn't knock down the door to save our relationship. It was over, no going back.

For three years I got on with my life finding my confidence as a single girl. I carried on with my sports and took a lover or two. One man captured my heart but our lives were so far apart that it could not last. It wasn't until 41 that I met a man I then fell for hook, line and sinker. A 6ft German, four and a half years my junior. We met windsurfing and he was almost a polar opposite to Tony. He rushed at me like a steam train and within five weeks he declared his love and that he would marry me. We had our ups and downs, but we enjoyed the same things and wanted the same things. He wanted a family.

Within weeks I knew I was pregnant and he did too; we were excited. He said to imagine how beautiful our children would be. Then not long after that, on Valentine's Day, we took a trip to Blackpool near where his new job would be (he was an engineer). Marco was a careless man with gusto and enthusiasm I could not describe. He dragged me through a fountain and as I slipped heavily I shattered my wrist. I quickly decided to have a metal plate inserted, and as I went down for the operation the anaesthetist asked if I could be pregnant, to which I replied yes. He looked shocked. He said, 'But you still want to go through with this operation, don't you?' There was no question, and I said yes.

Within two weeks I lost my child. I remember thinking at the time, 'I know we can get pregnant, so it will be OK'. We never did again. Over the next four years I learned more about fertility. I only wished I could have known the implications of so many things so much earlier. On reflection I vaguely recall my mother mentioning her periods stopped at 39. It didn't really register in my head and I knew little about daughters mirroring their mother's fertility clock. I never ever thought about the implications of this information for my own decisions.

In the first round of IVF I was as pragmatic as ever. I was told I had a 2% chance of falling pregnant with my rate of fertility, but I had to try. I also only had a 15% chance of carrying to term due to another surgeon's decision to remove most of my cervix. They extracted six eggs but none good enough to be fertilised.

We quickly turned to egg donation. The clinic recommended Cape Town, South Africa. I met the most amazing people along the way. The lady who would find me a donor has her own significant story, which touched my heart. What an amazing woman. She was determined to help other women who could not get pregnant naturally. She found a young lady,

Cade, who Marco said was just like me. We embarked on this process, following the clinic's instructions like a book. We were two weeks in Cape Town when Marco had my engagement ring made. It felt like I would finally have the family I was seeking: an amazing man who loved me and a beautiful child. But it was not to be. When we came back to London the first results were positive, but the follow up wasn't.

We could not face going through it all again so soon, so we decided to take a break for a while. We had five viable embryos in the clinic so could try later; but events turned again. By November Marco was about to lose his job and he said we should give up trying. I understood his stress and that he wanted to start his own business. It was natural I would support him emotionally and financially. I thought perhaps once he was more settled we could try again. But we broke up within months; his love for me had changed and I so desperately felt he was using me and had no intention of staying with me once his business took off. Some things are just not to be. Our frozen embryos remain in the Cape Town clinic to this day. The deep cut got deeper still as I learned within two months of us finally breaking up that Marco and another girl back in Germany were to have a child together.

My life felt so desperately sad and empty. Alone, single, miles from home and never to have a family of my own. I kept my grief hidden and never spoke of it to anyone. I did not want judgement or pity. I was ashamed, in a way, that I was not able to have a child. I have experienced the loss of people who meant so much to me in life, but I never understood the validity of this grief until I read Jody's article one day on the BBC website a year after Marco left.

The pain came flooding out as I read her words… 'Come and join your tribe'.

I do not know what my purpose is, but I do know that there is so much love inside of me that I will make an impact in at least one person's life, somewhere, one day.

Gateway girls, you *are* my tribe, and Jody is our rock, our matriarch.

What did you find hard when you realised

that you would not be a mother?

"It was sad, I felt cheated by something but not sure of what. I had always thought it would happen like it does in the films…"
Lucia

"I suppose it was hard to give up the hope that had dictated and took over my life for twelve+ years. It was always there in the background and letting go of that hope was the final stab at my heart. I also found it hard to talk to others because of the shame, guilt, lack of being a woman etc…"
Sam

"After years of enduring tortuous feelings it was a relief when I realised I won't have children. I had 'unexplained infertility' so there was never any end to the hope I might get pregnant. I've never been pregnant in my life so it became increasingly unlikely as the years ticked by that I ever would. I'm no longer trapped in time with the cycle of hope and grief as my companions…"
April

AN UNTOLD STORY

Nathalie, 43, Single

I had a collection of little books and would pick one for mum or dad to read to me every night. I had always imagined that one day it would be my turn to read bedtime stories too.

When your best mate excitedly shares with you the news of her pregnancy, you should feel happy too, shouldn't you? I wasn't. I was in tears. At the time, I was 34, single, feeling broody and it was painfully dawning on me that my dream of having kids and a family of my own just wasn't happening. What was wrong with me? On the surface, nothing. I was your average woman, well educated and financially independent, with a PhD, a good job, a loving family and a small number of very good friends. Underneath, however, I was plagued with low self-esteem, suffering from social anxiety and regular bouts of depression. Finding 'the dad' felt like mission impossible to me. As a woman, I felt like an utter failure.

Now 43, I have remained single and childless. Over the years, I have tried to put on a brave face in front of family, friends and colleagues, getting on with my life as best as I could, leaving the subject carefully undiscussed. Having to continuously put a mask on, I have felt increasingly isolated and disconnected from everybody. Joining the Gateway Women Plan B mentorship programme this year has helped me to peel away one layer after another of concealed sadness, pain, loneliness, isolation, regrets and shame. Finding this wonderful tribe of women, sharing their experiences and their own struggles, through tears and laughter, is allowing me to let go of the past and let myself 'be': a new me, true to myself.

As a child, my parents would read me a bedtime story every day. I had a collection of little books and would pick one for mum or dad to read to me every night. These moments were among the happiest and the most precious of my childhood. I had always imagined that one day it would be my turn to read bedtime stories too. So I had kept the books, always refusing to pass them on to other relatives or give them away to charity. This year I have decided to put them in a pretty box, along with other mementos of my life, so that they are no longer a sad reminder of 'what cannot be' but of cherished moments from the past, and just some of many memories to come.

Today my best friend told me over the phone **she is pregnant**. I don't want to loose a very good friend but I am really **worried about** how I am going to manage seeing her without **falling apart**.

Nathalie

THE LOST RELATIVE

Joanna, 47, Living with partner

"She is in fact obsessed with family trees! But
her fervour to reclaim lost relatives has become
the painful accompaniment to my yearning to
produce a family of my own."

My eyes glaze over and I zone out as my mother delivers yet another over-excited monologue about another long-lost relative she has discovered while investigating the mystery of her grandmother's paternity. This is just one of the many monologues of enthusiastic revelations she has delivered over a period of several years trying to unearth the missing branches of her own and others' family trees.

She is in fact obsessed with family trees! But her fervour to reclaim lost relatives has become the painful accompaniment to my yearning to produce a family of my own. And as she speaks, I compose the letter of revelations that will put an end to OUR family tree once and for all.

I am the younger of two daughters and now aged 43. My elder sister, who is five years older than me, is also childless. I have just finished my fifth IVF attempt and it's over three years since a 'simple' medical procedure that was supposed to restore my health instead left me with confusing and debilitating symptoms that no doctor seems able to diagnose accurately, let alone fix.

I have kept my fertility treatments secret from my mum, partly through shame of coming to the table late in the day and partly because I cannot bear to get her hopes up with each attempt, only to disappoint us both each time I fail to deliver. Her disappointment seems more unbearable than mine, perhaps because she is nursing my dad through a rapid deterioration from a neurodegenerative condition that will destroy him within three years.

My desire for children has incubated into a desperation to bring new life into my precipitously declining nuclear family. To create the next generation before the old one dies out. To give birth to a future before we face the loss of the present. Perversely, a missed miscarriage at nine weeks keeps my hopes alive and muzzles the voice of fear and doubt. I do not mourn my lost child – there is no time. I interpret the miscarriage as a sign that the dream IS possible and is meant to be. If not this time – with the right approach, enough attempts – surely soon?

But my body knows otherwise and throws me one curveball after another, while the yoke of yearning gets heavier with each failed attempt and each new baffling health development for both me and my dad. By the end of attempt five, I am ground to a halt, physically too ill to continue with either my own eggs or donated ones.

When weekend workshops on adoption and surrogacy overwhelm me, I acknowledge that hope is dying. We are unlikely to qualify for adoption, with my partner and I now coping with significant medical conditions, and surrogacy seems precarious in this country and financially exclusive in the States. And anyway, my fight and my body's energy are dwindling, as I am forced to admit that I would not have the stamina to parent a child in the state I'm in.

In facing this full stop, the burden of holding on to the secret becomes too heavy. I need my mum to know that I tried, and how hard I tried – and that I tried for both my partner and me, and for her too.

When I write the letter revealing all of this, I remind her that she once told me that her biggest drive and ambition as a teenager was to have children of her own. I remind her of her dream and how lucky she was to have had her two children. And I ask her if she could try to let those children be enough for her, so that I might be released from the burden of having failed her as well as myself.

I tell her that when thwarted from having my own family I have questioned my validity, my significance, my purpose, my future and more than anything my sense of belonging. It places me on the outside of other people's lives looking in. And it's excruciatingly lonely. Couple it with the endurance test of chronic illness and it can at times feel like being in a parallel universe, on the other side of life as I knew it, with no map or doors to work out how to get back to solid ground.

On the evening the secret is out, my mum is so sorry and sad for the 'private hell' I've been through. She calls me 'darling girl' and says she will try to hug me better. But the next day it seems over for her, and she tidies my despair away with encouragements to walk in nature or to marvel at the small things in life. But there is no tidying away for me, as now is when the mourning really starts, a grief so encompassing that I fear that I will literally break. I try to 'outbusy' my pain or run away from it – but it's not possible to cut free from this empty shadow that threatens to suffocate the light.

When my dad dies seven months after the letter, in place of grief my mum starts on yet another fervent dig to root out more long-lost relatives, this time on my dad's side of the family. She excavates living cousins, and other relatives of relatives; loose connections from decades long gone and lives once lived.

Soon my younger cousins give birth and produce sons and daughters, great nephews and nieces, who become the new generation for my mum to delight in. But I can't delight; for me they are Christmas presents wrapped up in despair. Acting my way through family events, I feel alone and disenfranchised, hiding my grief again, only with the knowledge that it's not a secret any more.

She doesn't mention my loss… Perhaps it's too much to bear alongside her own? Perhaps she has moved on, or perhaps she doesn't know how?

So now my heart cries out silently to her.

'Please stop looking for any more lost relatives, mum. There's a lost and grieving one right in front of you who needs to come home.'

I know going forward that, no matter how hard she searches, the family jigsaw puzzle can never be complete – the most longed-for piece will always be missing and can *never* be found.

The year in which I turned forty,

I said goodbye to that dream.

And it was hard,

probably the most difficult period of

my life[5]

IN MY END IS MY BEGINNING[7]

by Anonymous, 59, Divorced

*"D*o you have children?*"* the young chiropodist treating me asked. I flinch when asked this question and try to answer with a little of the truth. *"It didn't happen, sadly"*. She then said, icy with sarcasm, *"Too busy having a career, were you?"* and shot me in the heart. We had just been talking pleasantly about her two little ones, and she knew I was a senior clinician, working nearby. To this day I regret not having reported her. I wish I had swung my feet off her table and told her that not only was I painfully childless, but I had lost my marriage, my job and any possibility of ever having children. I'd thought I'd lose my home and very nearly lost my mind. And that she should never, ever make such a cruel and

ignorant assumption about another woman, never mind her patient, again.

When I was 37 and my husband 33, I went to a fertility clinic, for some basic hormone investigations; the results were normal for my age, but I was prescribed Premarin to give an extra boost to my fertility. My husband was then investigated and found to have low count, low motility and high abnormal forms. Eventually we saw a spermatologist privately for assisted, but not high-tech, conception. We were also assessed and accepted for IVF. However, as we had a 92% chance of failure and, as a clinician, I well understood the risks to my health. At the time (1990s) some of the drugs were brand new and not yet well tested - and they replaced the ones that had caused bovine encephalitis in some fertility patients given IVF treatment in the 1980s. I didn't want to increase all sorts of unknown risks, especially given our poor chances. I had said to myself that if I'd not conceived by 42, then it was not to be. Little did I know how accurate my intuition was. The following year my husband began an affair and his behaviour became unacceptable on many fronts. I told him to leave and I fragmented horribly for the next two years.

Therefore, my grief was for many things all at the same time. It took another two years after that before I was functioning properly, four years in total. I cannot separate out my grief for my childlessness from all those other griefs. I was in no state to find another partner and I knew I couldn't take the risk of having children straight away even if I could conceive and I most certainly wasn't strong enough to be a single parent.

Given my age, that really was it. It was a good ten years of longing and sorrow for the child that I would never have. I used to flood with grief in the most everyday situations such as seeing a lovely family in the supermarket. A wonderfully wise older woman (my clinical supervisor) said to me that one day I'd stop haemorrhaging with grief at the drop of a hat and would be left with only a dull ache that I would carry to my grave. And that's exactly how it has been.

What has been especially hard is not feeling understood or supported by my family. My mother said many times that she never understood why people had fertility treatment, that they should just accept their fate, that she wasn't maternal, that having children was my father's idea. Of course I found this truly wounding but she made it clear she was not going to engage in discussion. My sister has two children but has no ability to empathise with me and, given the parenting we received, this is entirely understandable. One of my greatest life lessons is that I have received much deeper love and compassion from outside of my family (and how fortunate is that!) as well as learning that I am simply not ever going to have a conventional family. Years later I can see that at least I haven't handed down our family dynamics, however unconsciously, which is now a small comfort. What I desperately wanted from my own family was deep intimacy/empathy/compassion, recognition and inclusion. Through having my own children, I hoped to create a family with these qualities. Denied this a second time, the miracle is, without quite realising it, increasing emotional intelligence, partnership and collaborative relationship has become the focus of my work in our health-care organisations.

But that is not all there is: I have been incredibly fortunate to have work that I love, and all my creativity has been poured into that. There are so many ways to mother, as the childless Canadian analyst, Dr Marion Woodman has said. So many ways of nurturing others, watching them develop, grow in confidence and fly off in ways they hadn't dared to even think of. With terrific, empathic friends, some of them parents, some childless and some childfree, I have such rich intimacy in my life. Twenty years on, I am still astounded that I found another channel for all this love and inspiration - as if, in the end, the depth and length of my grief has transmuted into feeling profoundly satisfied with what I can give and for what I receive.

I'm starting to notice

more of the **good things**

around me

and am feeling **hopeful**

and (dare I say it!)

a little **excited** about

the future[5]

PHOTOGRAPHIC MEMORY

by Jody Day

This photo of me was taken when I was about three or four years old. I'm sitting on the back of the sofa at my Auntie's house, hard up against the slightly silky feeling wallpaper, wearing my best clothes. The professional photographer has just done pictures of my two cousins, and now it's my turn and I'm loving the attention. I look frankly into the eye of the lens, and smile with an openness that still jumps out of the frame. At some point, a couple of years later when I'm learning to write, I've written a caption for the photo in felt tip, which you can just see at the bottom of the frame, *at MY Auties* it reads. I haven't quite mastered spelling or capitalisation yet, but the importance of this photo, this moment, this memory is already of great importance to me. It was a day when I mattered.

Those who know me connect with this photo of me because, in many ways, I haven't actually changed all that much. Little Jody has the cheekiness, openness and willingness that are still hallmarks of my nature, although I lost sight of them during the worst years of my grief over my childlessness. In those years, this photo lived in a box in storage and there's no way I could have looked at it, at her; she was both my memory of how much my ex-husband loved this photo, and also a reminder of the hope I'd had for our future children. I have a photo of my own mother at about the same age that I treasure; I imagined giving the portrait of Little Jody to my own daughter one day too.

When I was a child, I wanted to be a writer when I grew up, and my desire to record my story can be seen in that early, clumsy captioning of the photo. Now that I'm out the other side of my grief and have fully embraced my life as a single, childless woman, I have this photo near where I write. Little Jody keeps an eye on me, and reminds me not to take life too seriously. I look at her and as well as delighting in her freshness and optimism, it also reminds me that she is me, and that although I don't have a little girl of my own to nurture and cherish, I can nurture and cherish the little girl who lives on as a part of me. Doing so has been key to my healing and also has enabled me to open my heart joyfully to the children that *are* in my life again.

I still have the same open and unafraid way of looking to the camera, and my fringe still gives me problems in exactly the same spot. And although I didn't get the chance to be a mother, I did become a writer. The honesty, vulnerability and compassion that I hoped to give to my daughter, I now give to life in other ways. And it's enough. It matters.

Jody Day is the Founder of Gateway Women, the global friendship and support network for childless women and the author of *Living the Life Unexpected: 12 Weeks to Your Plan B for a Meaningful and Fulfilling Future Without Children* (Bluebird, 2016) www.gateway-women.com

Not having children has given me the **opportunity** to take a step back and truly look at my self **to discover who I am**.

Yvonne

SO, DO YOU HAVE CHILDREN?

I n her book *Living the Life Unexpected*[1] Jody Day mentions
that the question often asked of women seems to be 'So,
have you got kids then?' or perhaps 'So, how old are yours
then?' No matter how the question is presented, it's an experience that can leave us feeling hurt or devalued as women.
I bet that all of us who have been there have wished that we
could have given 'the' answer that would have stopped that
person in their tracks.

During her workshops Jody sometimes does an exercise
where women write down on one index card what they say
when someone asks them if they have children, and on another
card what they *wish* they had the nerve to say if they're asked
the common follow-up question: 'Why not?'

Here is a selection of their answers:

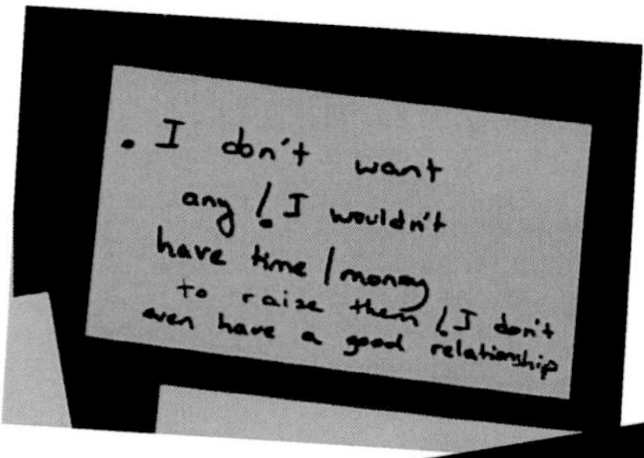
• I don't want any / I wouldn't have time / money to raise them / I don't even have a good relationship

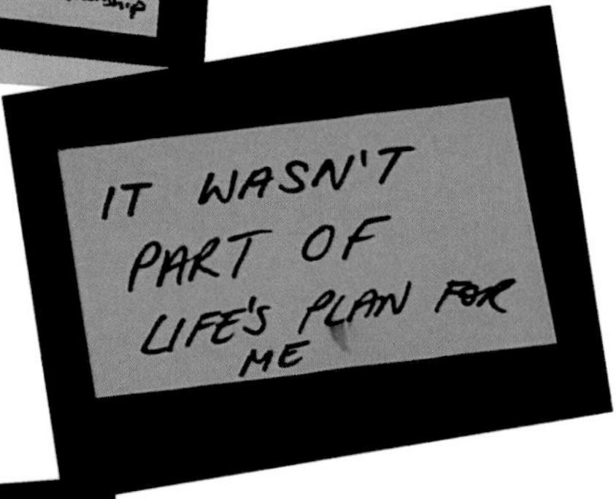
IT WASN'T PART OF LIFE'S PLAN FOR ME

YOU'VE TOUCHED A VERY RAW NERVE + I DON'T KNOW HOW TO RESPOND

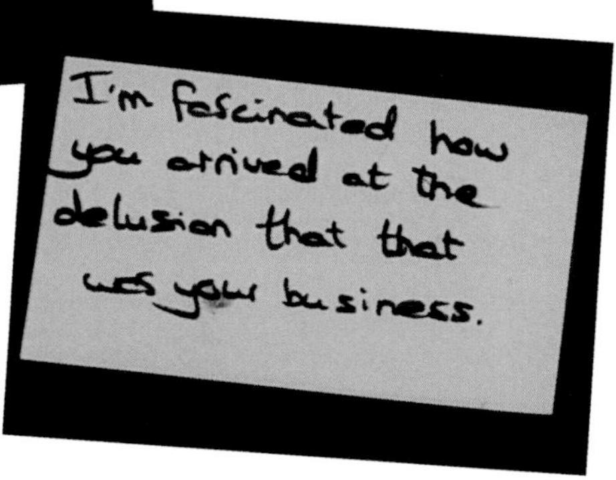
I'm fascinated how you arrived at the delusion that that was your business.

A DIFFERENT KIND OF LIFE

One of the biggest gifts that Gateway Women has given me is the sense of self-forgiveness. I had spent many years hiding from the truth of my past, feeling ashamed of what I perceived as mistakes. One termination seemed bad enough but almost forgivable at the time; but having to admit to two just felt enormous and all I could do was hide away from this shame. One of my most-used phrases became 'If they knew what I'd done, they wouldn't like me'. An older friend asked me when I was going to forgive myself. With the help of Jody Day (founder of Gateway Women and author of the bestselling Rocking the Life Unexpected: 12 Weeks to Your Plan B for a Meaningful and Fulfilling Life Without Children), I began to realise this was the only way I could move on from the grief of my past and of not being able to conceive. I remember my first one-to-one sessions with Jody where we explored the 'whys' of my decisions. It was the first time that I allowed myself to be so vulnerable without any judgement. It was the first time that I experienced a kindness that allowed me to explore my past, which in turn allowed me to understand my feelings and allowed me to just cry.

The 12-month plan B mentorship programme that I started in March 2015 began after I had attended a living without children workshop with Jody back in December 2014. It was a very emotionally confusing time as I had recently received my 'unexplained infertility' diagnosis and was having difficulties processing this information as well as the new emotions that came with it. I remember sitting in a room with around 11 other women and realising for the first time that I was not alone. Finally I could start to make sense of what I was going through. At times I felt like I was in the right place, and at times, because of my decisions to terminate my pregnancies, I felt that I didn't deserve to be there, but the one thing that I held on to was the fact that it hurt like hell to feel this pain and I needed to heal.

The biggest thing for me, upon joining the plan B programme, was that I was no longer alone. I had found a group of women who shared my feelings and understood what I was going through. We all have our own unique stories with one thing in common: we are grieving the loss of our unborn children. Finally my grief was recognised. Finally my grief was acknowledged. Together we are exploring our strengths and passions. Together we are holding each other's hands as we compassionately navigate our way through our grief while we explore our lives without children.

THE UNOPENED BOX

On my road to recovery I have met some wonderful women, women with heart-breaking and inspirational stories. I wish I could have included all of them in this book, but some were just not ready to allow the world to bear witness to this painful part of their lives and let their grief be seen. I dedicate this chapter to those women who are bravely working through their grief. Although their individual voices cannot be heard right now, their stories resonate in the stories in this book.

EPILOGUE

Today I heard someone say that wisdom and knowledge come from grief, which reminded me of how far I have come since the start of my journey. One of the things that I was afraid of when I started writing this book was my fear of how I would be judged for my past. The shame I carried with me for so long dominated my thoughts and actions. Working through my grief has helped me to look into my mirror and speak to myself with a kindness and understanding that I had never felt before. I learnt how to be compassionate to myself. This compassion has helped me to let go of my shame and has helped my marriage to grow in a way I would not have imagined it could have. It has helped me to be gentler to myself and to those around me. This compassion has helped me to truly love all of me.

Showing my vulnerability was not an easy road to take but now I have a new strength that guides and comforts me. I have learnt that my strength is in my vulnerability, and now that I own it I find it easier to be honest with the world around me.

Yvonne John – I Salute You!

When I first met Yvonne, there was an air of inner strength and a steely determination that she projected, although you had to look closely to see and understand it. Her warm smile, genuine and engaging, always draws people in.

When she asked if I would coach her to give birth to a book she was contemplating writing I was thrilled and felt privileged and delighted that she wanted to share her story not only with me, but with the whole world. The emotional travellator that she embarked on has changed her and me, and by sharing the most intimate part of her life anyone can imagine, the impact of her words on other women, men and young people will definitely bring about a lasting change for the better for all of us.

I am so proud to have been involved from the beginning of Yvonne's journey in bringing *Dreaming of a Life Unlived* to fruition. It was an insight and an honour to have taken her through the myriad personal layers of her life and the lives of the women who trusted us to share their own journeys within the book.

Coaching Yvonne was a delight. She fought through the most difficult sections of her life and pulled together the stories of the gutsy women who wanted to share their personal words. She went through a step-by-step process where she was questioned, she rose to the challenge and found a steely determination and inner strength that motivated her to have the courage to communicate to the world her honest truth. She pushed and was driven to tell her story; she was encouraged to be still and reflect and to dig deep into what she had to offer the world.

Dreaming of a Life Unlived is a book that tells the story of Yvonne's coming to terms with living without children and how the guilt she held onto for decades finally dissipated with the support from Gateway Women, family and friends. She found her voice to say 'I am ready to tell my story'.

She is the hero of the narrative shaping her destiny, and this book is a true reflection of the Yvonne who stepped up to the plate to be a woman of substance. She reveals the trauma, the shame, the embarrassment that she felt and how these strong feelings shaped her past life and could have shaped her future. How she passionately turned these feelings into strengths, honesty and courage is laced throughout the pages.

By reading this book you will come to understand the women who have shared in their own words what living without children is like for them, and the responses and lack of respect and under-standing they face from others, including the funny side and the sad side of what people think. But more importantly you will see how they have influenced, validated and in a positive way given hope to those who are going through their own similar journeys.

Yvonne, and the ladies who shared their stories, I salute you! My mission statement is:

'Learning to believe in yourself gives inner strength to achieve the impossible.'

Yvonne you have done it – well done!

Helen Tucker

Career Coach & Business Consultant

RESOURCES

1. Day, J 'Living the Life Unexpected: 12 Weeks to Your Plan B for a Meaningful and Fulfiling Future without Children' by Jody Day (2016) Bluebird, Pan Macmillan

2. www.gateway-women.com/

3. Walsch, N D, Conversations with God

4. http://ivf.cliniccompare.co.uk/cost-of-ivf-treatment-in-the-uk

5. The Lone Bee [Blog]. www.thelonebee.com/ (Accessed: October 2015)

6. Finding my Plan B [Blog]. www.findingmyplanb.wordpress.com/

7. Mary, Queen of Scots embroidered these words in Latin, echoing Isaiah 46:10, on her Cloth of Estate when held in prison by her cousin Elizabeth I. http://marie-stuart.co.uk/Mariaregina.htm